Book of Life

ONE LINERS TO LIVE BY

DEVENDRA JAIN

A Person of Few Words

Illustrated by:
TARINI URVEE NEEAL

Here is a book that starts with a grand daughter
and granddad celebrating life which ends with an
obituary by one and exhortation to keep learning
by the other.

WHY A BALLET PICTURE ON THE COVER?
*because it embodies the spirit of
the book touching as many as
14 One Liners.*

I was all ears when my granddaughter was talking about a fathers and daughters ballet performance. I sensed an opportunity. I thought here was a challenge. So I asked her to check if grandfather could also join. I went on stage for the first time for a non-technical presentation. I was aware that one misstep and I could end up ruining my little partner's happiness. Every stage in life presents challenges from the early years until the last day. So I took up the challenge to be her partner.

Life needs commitment to tasks, small and big. Do not give up on your mental and physical abilities as you grow old. There were commitments to rehearsals both as a group and individually at home. In retrospect, it seems simple but some tasks seemed more important than going for a rehearsal.

Participation needed a can-do mindset. It is there in business all the time. In leisure, we tend to go easy. For me inspiration came from others, e.g., Fauja Singh who ran a marathon at 102. Have the courage to follow your heart. It was almost like learning to type in the UK at age 25 when all other students in the class were girls training to be a secretary and I was the only one looking into the future to be able to do his own typing.

Willingness to take the first step into the unknown. Learning a new skill, coordinated movement of hands, legs, and body. By accepting to be in this dance I made a promise. Accepted the challenge to do something that others feared to take up.

Help came from all around and in abundance from a guru who believed in me. Ms Nikolina accepted me for a group performance but along the way, she quietly changed my role to suit my learning limitations rather than drop me from the performance altogether. So I had this opportunity for a duet. And I competed with myself. Small wins gave me the courage to keep moving ahead.

Keep your eyes and ears open to find new opportunities!

ISBN 979-8-89233-945-2

Dedicated to

my parents,

whom I got to 'know' more after I started writing this book!!
Their contribution to my growth I realised more as each page of this
book was written. Specially the career path I chose to take.

Also, to my grandchildren
Diya, Amlaan, Tarini and Taanishi.

I am amazed to see them excel in their chosen fields of Endeavour.

Contents

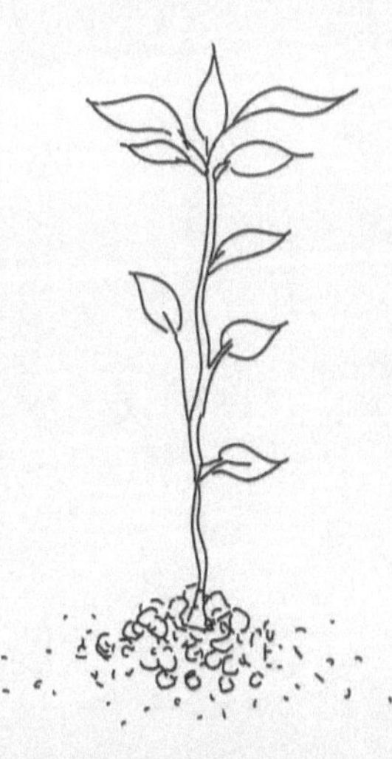

Foreword

As I sit down to write this foreword for my father's book, I am filled with a profound sense of pride and admiration. His life has been a journey marked by resilience, wisdom, and an unwavering commitment to his principles. In these pages, which I believe will help the youth of today, he has shared not just his experiences but the invaluable lessons he has garnered from them. These are what has built the business – Pluss Advanced Technologies, that exists today and he along with me and several others strived to turn it into an institution that can last beyond our lifetimes. These also determined how I and my sister were brought up!

The book is unlike any other book on how to run your life or business. It is what he followed diligently day in and day out and has captured it leaving it to, you,the reader to figure out what to adopt where in life.

As you browse these pages, you will find that his story demonstrates the value of hard effort, the significance of integrity, and the significance of timeliness. He weathered successes and hardships addressing adversity with steadfast commitment. Not coming from a business family, and starting a research and development led business based on innovations at a time when capital was never easily available, he found his own ways to grow the business without any external support. It had its challenges – the biggest being slow growth which I believe has been overcome recently with a strategic tie up with Carborundum Universal. These one liners tell you how you can be an intrapreneur if not an entrepreneur in your own company!

In every chapter of this book, I see reflections of his commitment to work that instills a sense of responsibility and an aim in life one should have to be able to achieve success. He was never vocal and shared moments of joy in private and with chosen few. His journey, from humble beginnings to current accomplishments, resonates with anyone seeking inspiration.

As readers delve into the single-liners that he accumulated over years, they will find not a story but a reservoir of insights—nuggets of wisdom that transcend time and circumstances. His way of thinking influencing, and guiding us through the complexities of life and urging us to embrace the beauty of the human life force, that allowed us to create a small organisation, Pluss, based on value. He distinguished between money and wealth. Wealth is what we leave behind for generations to grow further.

It is my hope that others will be as moved, inspired, and grateful for the lessons within these lines that you, my father, have followed throughout your life.

Thank you, for sharing your lessons, for being an inspiration of strength, and for teaching us that a life well-lived is a story worth telling.

With love and pride,

Samit
Gurgaon, INDIA

Thank you,

Priyanka, for having efficiently converted my notes on scraps of paper into a readable manuscript.

Vidya Viswanathan for editing and improving my English presentation.

Anil Mehta, Atul Baijal and other business colleagues who pointed out some errors of date to make the narration more accurate.

Dr Harshita Mittal for our extensive discussion on how we should approach promotion of the book.

Samit for silently backing up my efforts, Neeraj and Alpana for vocally encouraging me to continue. Charu who one day quietly picked up the manuscript before it went to the publisher and honed the presentation including dividing the book into sections, a tough job considering that many One Liners overlap each other in what they convey.

Thank you to Ms Nikolina of Nikolna Nikoleski Dance Academy, New Delhi for permission to publish cover picture.

Finally thank you Rajat and Manjari of Twig Designs for the Book Design.

What is this book about?

I have come across one liners all through my life starting from the time
when I was a child. My mother would say *'Boond-boond kar ke ghada bhar
jata hai'* (drop by drop a bucket fills up). It could refer to saving money at
every opportunity, saving water, saving time, or accumulating anything else.
Depending upon what the context was we understood what it meant. We did
not need any more explanations.

Today, there are thousands of such phrases, also referred to as proverbs.
A single line at a time is a treasure of wisdom shared by generations gone
by. Whenever I encountered such an intense dose of wisdom and it made
sense to me in my own way of looking at life, I made a note. This book is a
presentation of part of that collection with my own occasional comments.
I read a lot. So, I stood on the shoulders of the learned people gone by, for the
wisdom in this collection. I owe them debt starting with my mother Vidya and
at a different level my father, Madan Mohan.

This collection is thus a life story with a difference. All through my life from
1966 onwards, I made notes of what I learned as time went on. When I looked
back 56 years later, on what my life had been, a very interesting fact emerged.
The notes when edited turned out to be just like one-line proverbs. Some of
these were adapted from ages-old proverbs and some quotes from learned
men and women in history over centuries. There are others that are simple
facts of life but with profound truth in practice. Looking at them collectively,
it turns out, that these were the principles that made my life. It is not an
autobiography.

These One Liners stand like guiding pillars small and big, in a circle where
none can be marked first. The reader can start and finish anywhere. Practicing
the one-liners as compiled in this collection has allowed me to live a fulfilling
life. The book has only broad sections because learning in life happens
randomly. Some come as one-liners from books read over the years, just
one thought from a whole book. This presentation is my collection of such
thoughts from over the last 55+ years. Analysis has shown me that these One
Liners have been guide posts in my life - personal and business.

Even today I can open the book at any point and look in any direction and get
guidance. The result is that I can say with confidence that when the end of my
life comes I will not have to say "I wish I had done..."

Starting out

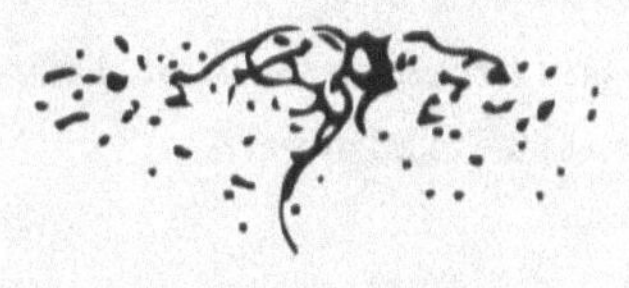

A Vedic Hymn.

Look to this day,

For it is life, the very life of life,

In its brief course lie all the realities and verities of
existence……

Today well lived

Makes every yesterday a dream of happiness, and

Every tomorrow a vision of hope

Look well, therefore, to this day.

Every morning
I have an opportunity
to change!

Look in the mirror every morning and decide what
am I going to be doing today that fits in with *"if it is
the last day ……"*

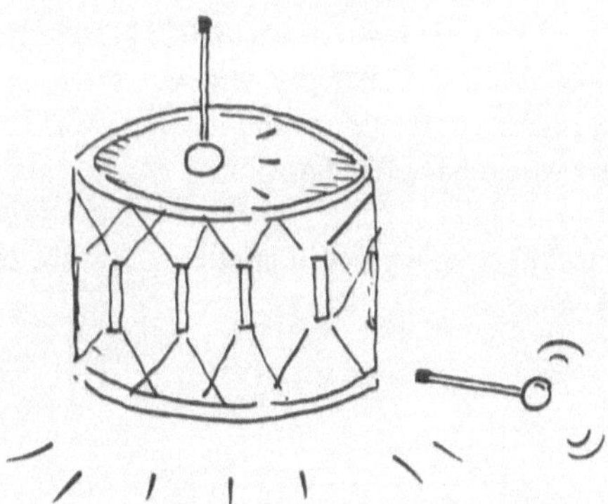

You have to find
your own path to peace.

Over the last half a century or so I have found peace in

- A visit to a library,

- Buying books

- A visit to IHC and

- Eating a snack at one of the few of my favourite places such as the IHC library lounge.

I strongly recommend to everyone to have such a favourite place of your own. There would be times when no one is available to celebrate your successes.

Don't give up
on your mental and physical abilities
as you grow old.

Visit to Mumbai – 09-03-21 evening to 16-03-21 evening.

I was apprehensive of travelling alone.

What would Covid restrictions be like at the airports? And other associated norms. Walking around with the mask was a minor inconvenience. It would remind me that I was not totally free to live life as I would have liked to.

But I was pleased that I still have the ability to travel on my own. Thank you, God.

Schooling/Childhood:
Make the most of what life brings to you.

We were not rich. I would go to *'Kabaadi'* shops at Jama Masjid, Delhi to find used/second hand machine parts for tinkering and producing my craft models - they were always mechanical contraptions.

This it seems was part of that learning which allowed me to experiment a lot with limited resources. My father supported me with an occasional book such as Boy Electrician. A collection of projects for boys in secondary schools. In retrospect, 65 years back there was clear demarcation of what boys and girls could do. I had another book which had drawings for building a model ship in wood. I tried but could not finish. I did try to make an airplane model. It was a propeller-based model. The propeller worked with energy stored in a rubber band twisted by turning the propeller. There were a few other things I did during the time I was an undergraduate student at Delhi University (1958 to 1961).

Growing up – my parents gave me freedom to choose my field of study. Accepting and encouraging me to work in kitchen. Freedom to tinker with things and thus my growth in technology.

Accepting my 2nd divisions in School & College and University without a reprimand (unheard of in those days).

"

I have a right to dream.

I dream of the 21st century.

The century that belongs to India.

Let us make it happen. Start today.

It can be done.

Dreams do come true.

Just excel in whatever we do.

And you will see things take shape.

This applied to my life. August 1999.

If you want to get a job done, ask the busiest person around.

From my *babuji's* (father's) time, around 1958, when I was the go-to person for all small odd jobs at home.

And later on I found that a busy person usually is also one who is more efficient in organising their time.

I am a great believer in luck and I find the harder I work the more I have of it.

-Thomas Jefferson

Dream is not what you see in sleep. OL 9

Dream is the thing which does not let you sleep.

– A P J Abdul Kalam.

Work hard on any task that you take up. OL 10

I am sure everyone works as hard as they can but in innovation
there are so many unknowns that I add 'luck' as the last line before
summing up. I take care not to cheat myself.

I need to be a hard task master for my behaviour and hence these
repetitions.

You have to dream first
before your dreams can come true!

Here is an apocryphal story.

A devotee had been praying to God regularly for years with no results. One day he got really angry with the God and shouted *"Oh God, I have been so devoted to you but years have gone by and you gave me nothing. Get me at least a lottery!"*. Suddenly the god appeared and said *"at least go and buy a lottery ticket first"*.

All dreams start with your immediate past experiences. Some may relate to what happened the day before or in the near past. When you dream for future, it still has its beginning in the present or the immediate past. Is it ok to dream? I am all for it. When you want something badly and the dream stays with you, you will work towards achieving it. Needs are fulfilled for all (to their level of needs). But it is the wants that grow you. Wanting something badly gets you into action for achieving that.

It took me about 21 years before I took a concrete step towards achieving my dream of starting a business in 1982. See more about it in "How I Started My Business". (Book of Life Part 2, yet to come).

Sometimes there will be people, a good friend, your spouse or someone else who will encourage and help you achieve your dreams but often it is the dreaming which keeps your energy focused into achieving what you want to get.

Authority is grabbed as the occasion arises. It is not given. OL 12

In a lab or even office what I found happens is that you gently overstep your limits and offer to help other people. At some point your acumen will get noticed. In due course the word will spread that you are the go-to person to get the job done.

Some colleagues would not want any interventions then you simply step aside. I then make sure that I was in no way trying to grab any credit that belonged to the other person. That is never the aim.
In fact, I would make conscious effort to stay out of the way and try not to seek any credit.

The more you play this game, the more authority and freedom gets given to you.

Suddenly, one day you will have that coveted promotion.

Achieving a long-term goal needs Grit! OL 13

Grit is passion and perseverance for long term goal. Grit is living life like a marathon and not a sprint. Talent does not make you gritty.

When you know how brain changes as you learn, you are more likely to continue because you know failure does not mean growth will stop.

- Angela Duckworth in a Ted Talk.

In your early years acquire knowledge and experience as if there may not be a tomorrow.

Now that I started writing my experiences, I keep coming face to face with so many ways I acquired knowledge. At that time, it was simply inquisitiveness but after a couple of decades all this keeps coming back to me as helpful learning.

During a visit (school holidays) around mid-1950s to the orchards of my *Mausiji*. I experienced what horticulture and food processing is all about. They processed and packed in tins mangoes at *Ajitmal*, a small village in Etawah district. Back home I tried bottling green peas in brine. Learnt how to make an airtight seal with wax on water top and many other processing tricks.

I joined photography club in my first year of B.Sc. at Delhi University which exposed me to a lot of photography tricks and experience in developing and printing of negatives and positives.

It gave me experience in estimation scale for light exposure of photographic paper while printing and shading by manual movement of a tiny Obstruction in the passage of light to make lighter shade. It was all black and white. Needed controlled movements and fine estimates in a dark room with minimal red light to feel my way around.

I also learnt carpentry at the Delhi University Hobby Workshop. This included working on a lathe. There were no other students interested in this kind of learning so I had all the attention from *Panditji*, the instructor.

You need money when you are young but......

Everyone needs money so did I, and you need it when it is most in short supply. When you are young.

Despite such a situation I made it a point to save a small amount from the salary I received each month and also make a donation for a good cause every year. There are always people less fortunate than me drawing no salary.

There is always a view that they ought to work or work harder. But I would share a bit from what I have. Once I was a few years older I started saving for a time when old age would dictate that I stop working. Today at 80+, I look back and feel good. You need money when you are young but need it more when you are older.

Luck favours the well prepared. I didn't know these big words .... But I took a risk.

Went to UK on a one-way ticket but with good preparations for finding a job once I landed there in November 1965. *Babuji* advised me to locate possible jobs by scanning ads in local (British) newspapers at British Council Library, New Delhi. I applied by airmail giving my date of arrival in UK and a local address.

When I got there, I had a few interview calls awaiting me. In fact, I got three jobs within a month to choose from. – luck favours the well prepared!

Opportunity is missed by most people because it is dressed in overalls and looks like work.

-Thomas Edison

Take risks in life. The bigger the better, but wisely taken.

Take risks in life. The bigger the better. Calculated risks, wisely taken. Look at worst case scenario.

Invest/saturate the actions with all that is available to you (resources). If you succeed, the resulting enjoyment will know no bounds. If you fail, there is always a next time. But no foolhardy venture. Have at least one more person's concurrence.

Everybody including you yourself remember successes. What you are today is because of your accumulated successes. Why burden the mind by going over the failures again and again? Have your own strong moral principles to back up your moves. It applies both to personal and business life.

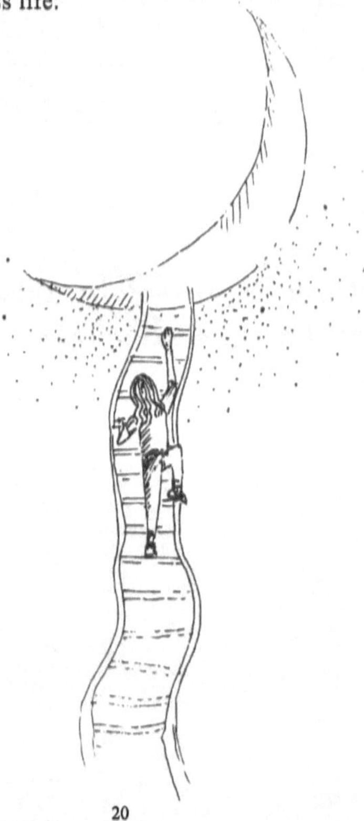

Take Risks after exploring worst case scenario.

Depending upon the risks being taken, more or less thinking will be involved. In all cases I had pros and cons of the decision written out. Always. If not done this way mind plays the tricks and magnifies risks or gains disproportionately and you may end up taking the wrong alternative. By writing down there are tricks you can use to eliminate 'unforeseen' shocks.

At every step-in life, you need to take risks. Returns are always related to the degree of risk. Higher the risk the bigger the returns. The caveat is that the action has to be well thought out and not be foolhardy. Always explore the worst-case scenario. See that it is compatible with your life's plan. Can you bear the shock, should it turn out to be the reality? I chose to take many risks in life. They were all well considered. Never reckless.

Some that come to mind immediately are:

a. Choosing to join SRIFIR as a junior research fellow in 1963 rather than a better paid job elsewhere.

b. Go to England in Nov 1965 on a one-way ticket.

c. Deciding to marry Tripti and waiting until parents saw my point of view and agreed in 1968. A promise kept. See OL39.

d. Taking up part time studies for polymer technology while in England (1966).

e. Return to India in 1970 for the love of the country and its culture.

f. Quitting the ICI job in favour of starting my own business (1982).

Since the decision to start a business there have been numerous risks that I have taken. Initially the risks were taken after discussion with whoever I could tap for brainstorming/advice. But majorly Tripti and my father.

More on risk taking. Support from libraries.

As time went on, the major contributing factor has been my extensive studies of varied subjects through use of various libraries starting in 60s. such libraries included school, college, and university libraries. Also important were British Council, Central Secretariat and Delhi Public libraries. When I knew what risk taking is, my first instance of having to deicide for or against taking the risk to go to England came in 1965. Never once did my parents make any remarks that would mean avoid taking risk of going to a foreign land. In the long run this turned out to be my finest years, in that early period.

Again, most people discouraged us from returning to India in 1970 but this decision also turned out to be a great step which gave me a lot of learning that would prepare me for the eventual launch of my own business, in 1982. That entailed much greater risk taking. In brief, small wins give you tremendous confidence of taking ever bigger risks and grabbing more opportunity.

Another of my favourite Quotes is *"Lady luck dances with those who are already on the dance floor"*. So be there to grab the opportunity when the time comes.

Life can only be understood backwards but it must be lived forward.

My formative years:

Life can only be understood backwards but it must be lived forward. So, I decided to put some more parts of my personal and professional life as a section here.

Professionally my formative years were spent in England at ICI's Petrochemicals and Polymers Lab under the guidance of Dr Isaac Goodman.

Isaac was one of the senior scientists there. I was lucky to be assigned to him. Normally, a Ph.D works for a person of that level. So, I got some great learning opportunities from him. Other people working for him were 3 Britons (all with Ph.Ds from US).

By association, therefore, my status went up. I had some early success that in a way established me there as a competent chemist. Unlike most other universities in India at that time, Kurukshetra was the only one that taught polymer science in MSc (Dr H.L. Bhatnagar). I understood macromolecules well. One of Isaac's teams was trying to synthesize an oligomer from caprolactone and hexamethylene diamine. Working for months they did not succeed. The preparation of the monomer had been described in a Union Carbide patent. But the team could not replicate it.

One day Isaac nonchalantly handed me the problem to see if I could do something. I put aside the melt condensation method that they were following and reasoned:

- If this is so highly reactive a monomer, I should carry out the reaction at low temperatures.

- Further to reduce rate of reaction I should do it in a solution.

I therefore, made molar solutions of the two monomers. Made it dilute. Mixed. Left it overnight at room temperature. What I found next morning was amazing – crystals of the required oligomers. It was characterised and so on. Later I could just mix the two monomers at low temperature. Gradually raise the temperature and get a 100% yield where none was possible for a long time. Such instances helped me in establishing myself as a polymer chemist.

Simultaneously, in those years I took a 3-year polymer technology course which gave a fillip to my understanding of polymers in practical uses. A combination that not many had at that time. (ref. OL 12) In my journey through the years, I had many such challenges. Each one reinforced my spirit and belief that I am capable of doing innovations.

All progress depends upon the unreasonable man.

OL 22

"The reasonable man adapts himself to the world. The unreasonable one persists in trying to adapt the world to himself"

– G B Shaw

First quoted to me by my colleague Tripathi at CAFI in 1972.

Sharing failures is as important as sharing successes.

Having read the book 'Better' by Atul Gawande, a surgeon, I decided I would share my failures every time one happens with all who are around, in the hope that I would get some quick help from one or more of my colleagues. This openness does cause some embarrassment but I am not perfect and help is welcome.

Here are my failures of last week (story is some years old):

a. I theorised and we made a Reinforced-form stable PCM with OM32 and 10-50 mm length acrylic fibres. But it does not work! Fibres are highly entangled and do not spread when making a Compression Moulded Sheet.

b. I failed to teach two of my assistants how to control temperature of a compression moulding press or for that matter any other equipment. I taught it again and again.

(**Toyota way**: if a student has not learnt, the teacher has not taught).

I believe sharing failures will help us grow faster since similar mistakes are avoided in future. I encouraged all my colleagues to do that.

How to find an opportunity?

Simple,

Keep your eyes and ears open!

Opportunity is always disguised. It is your constant alertness that will allow you to catch an opportunity.

I need to be scared of ... well, things going wrong. OL 25

Failure in business decisions (a decision turning out to be wrong), breaking a law, and its consequences for my future. Money & time wasted to manage the situation in future. I need a teacher.

Fear in appropriate dose is a great teacher that forces me to think of alternatives for any situation. "Appropriate dose" are the operating words, you discover this appropriate amount as time goes on. God is also for me an 'image' to focus on when I need to concentrate my energies in specific directions. Be scared of God (a force beyond human understanding). I need God to be able to attribute all that I don't understand and thereby move on in life. It is like finding a scapegoat for my own actions.

Do not carry work home. OL 26

Keep work and home life separate. I also give younger people of today a contradictory advice. 9 to 5 work will not get you far in today's world where people are trying to do more in each day that comes by. Well, more time for work depends upon many factors. Type of work, the environment, your own expertise in handling the job at hand. What I found useful was to work longer in office but never carry papers home, for example, to work an hour after dinner.

Work at home means working at lower efficiency and vitiating the home atmosphere for all others at home.

Problems in relationship —
use a pen & paper to start on
finding a solution.

It is difficult to solve an emotional problem by talking about it verbally. The mind keeps prevaricating when anyone believes he/she is adversely affected by a certain point of view. It is true that if there is a grievance one party will be affected more than the other.
To minimize this, I have found, repeatedly, a pen and paper is the best bet on finding a solution quickly Or at least to find out where you stand on the issue and then be prepared to make compromises. It is superbly applicable when you are alone and there is no one available to brainstorm or seek advice from.

The starting point is to define the problem in as few words as possible. Then have two columns. In one write your own views – not in prose but as bullet points. See the points are not repeated. In the second column write views of the other person. If possible, opposite your own relevant view. Then see how the two sides can compromise – in the process you become an unbiased umpire. After a while you will have the solution.

It is the best solution, if the other person does not accept the solution, that is their problem. Not quite, but then go for a compromise as best as you can.

However, out of love & relationship you may want to give up some of your rights/advantages. But that is as they say you are being more than fair in trying to come to an amicable solution.

How far back do you go to balance the equation? May be 1 year, 2 years, 10 years. Decide before starting the analysis.

Learn at least one more language, other than English and you mother tongue.

Tripti never forced me to learn Bangla, but boasted before others that I could speak the language. In reality I could read, write but speak to rudimentary level. Because I had made enough efforts to learn so much that I could get by in a totally Bangla speaking environment. Script especially helps sharpen certain faculties in the brain.

Speaking other person's language is sure to win their heart. I discovered it both in Germany and Bengal. I even tried Tamil/French/Russian but the drive to learn vanished as the need to learn the language vanished. I believe a new script especially help sharpen certain faculties in the brain.

Do not be afraid to make mistakes, ...

but never the same mistake twice.

Demand the finest from your assistants and you will almost get it.

There is an artificiality here. They do certain things under threat of pain (consequences of not doing what the boss/company wants).

If you could be outspoken – call a spade a spade. You will have less mental baggage to carry and progress faster. I have followed this approach. Having courage of conviction is tough but a great virtue.

In a nutshell – keep your promise. Have courage of conviction.

Once in life do fall in love.

- Swapan Seth

Once in life do fall in love, not necessarily with a person but with an idea, a dream, the faith, an ambition. More often it will be a reason to wake up with a smile every morning.

If you are the smartest person in the room, then you are in the wrong room.

- Confucius.

I want to be sure that I also have company of people smarter than me.

Remain accessible to all at work.

Generally, anywhere but especially in India junior most level workers are reticent about talking to their bosses. They feel intimidated by the difference in levels. I have had some wonderful and confidential insights from lower-level workers about the working of the factory.

I am careful not to encourage them beyond a point so that they do not feel privileged, and I begin to get distorted picture.

They even reported a theft from the factory to me rather than the security office. Because they could trust me to keep informant's identity confidential. The theft was by the General Manager!

How did these One Liners help me get to my destination?

It is not a biography but a guide for younger people to get to where I am and beyond; you have the benefit of my experience! Just keep your eyes and ears open and you have all the wisdom to grab from around you.

This book will guide you to imbibe what is important. The book presents what I heard, saw, read and practiced. This is something which is within the realm of everyone.

How does this process start? I do not know the one way! But there are many indicators.

Read, Read, and Read more. Buying books is not a substitute for a library, but do buy as ....

I became a member of Delhi Public Library when I was in school. My favourite method of using a library now is to stand in front of a bookshelf, chosen randomly and run my eyes over the spines of a row of books. Almost invariably I would come across a book which I would not have seen in a bookstore. The stores only keep what are popular/fast moving titles.

Holistic living

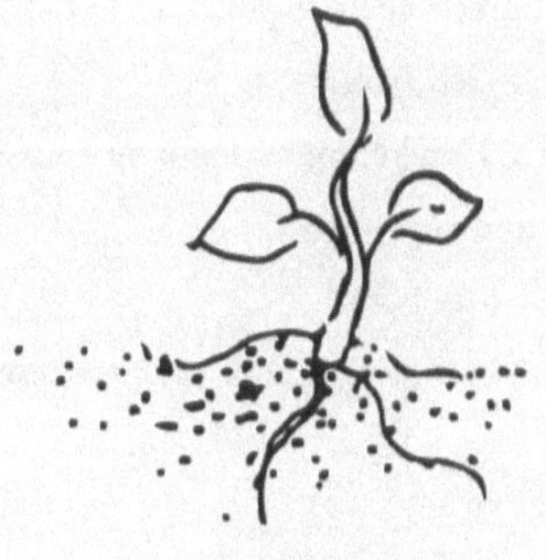

OL 34 Think of alternatives for any situation before the need arises.

OL 35 You have to be on the dance floor first for Lady Luck...

OL 36 Chance favours only the prepared mind.

OL 37 Value of Technology and financial Investment in...

OL 38 You will win when no stakeholder in the transaction loses...

OL 39 I Promise.

OL 40 Give someone a small gift or a hand written note...

OL 41 Training of the mind (TOM).

OL 42 Do not spend your time on the low-level choices. Save time!

OL 43 Live a minimalist life style.

OL 44 Do not have strong likes and dislikes. My belief.

OL 45 Don't wish it were easier. Wish you were better.

OL 46 Do not waste your time on comparing yourself with...

OL 47 Look at and examine in detail the worst-case scenario...

OL 48 Stumble at times – But get up and keep walking again.

OL 49 Get small wins, celebrate.

OL 50 Small wins give you courage to keep moving.

OL 51 Look for small wins and these together will make...

OL 52 Indira Nouyi said - Don't feel like that you have to...

OL 53 Need Vs. Want Vs. Desire.

OL 54 Ask an unstructured question and you could get...

OL 55 Call a spade a spade.

OL 56 Leave every place a little better than how you found it...

OL 57 When you get fed up of being fed up, you will change.

OL 58 If you cheat yourself or lie to yourself, not even God...

OL 59 Stop cheating myself (yourself).

OL 60 Trust but verify. Can you put a hand on your heart and...

OL 61 Keep my eyes and ears open.

OL 62 I want to be my own boss.

OL 63 Will not take a revenge any more than the damage the...

OL 64 **No revenge.**

OL 65 **As a principle in my business, we are more than fair to...**

OL 66 **Am I afraid of God? For what it might do to me or...**

OL 67 **Get to know your parents; you never know when they...**

OL 68 **The myth of quality time.**

OL 69 **Respect your elders.**

OL 70 **Being a parent is tough.**

OL 71 **Advice is a form of nostalgia trying to do, through your...**

OL 72 **Don't be reckless with other people's heart.**

OL 73 **Breaking the rules. Do unto others as you would have...**

OL 74 **Do not give up if you believe a child needs to be protected...**

OL 75 **It is better to have loved and lost than to have never...**

OL 76 **छिमा बड़न को चाहिये, छोटन को उत्पात**

OL 77 **Happiness or joy. Be with people for life rather than for...**

OL 78 **You should be joyful by yourself and not because of...**

OL 79 **Long-term relationship needs tolerance.**

OL 80 **Don't do anything today that you will be ashamed of...**

OL 81 **Character is doing the right thing when no one is watching!**

OL 82 **Some valuable advice from my wife!**

OL 83 **Trust but verify.**

OL 84 **Make a promise and believe in it.**

OL 85 **Adding life in my years.**

OL 86 **Live each day as if it is your last day.**

OL 87 **Someone asked – what is forgiveness?**

Think of alternatives for any situation before the need arises.

It is difficult to solve an emotional problem by talking about it verbally. The mind keeps prevaricating when anyone believes he/she is adversely affected by a certain point of view. It is true that if there is a grievance one party will be affected more than the other.
To minimize this, I have found, repeatedly, a pen and paper is the best bet on finding a solution quickly Or at least to find out where you stand on the issue and then be prepared to make compromises. It is superbly applicable when you are alone and there is no one available to brainstorm or seek advice from.

The starting point is to define the problem in as few words as possible. Then have two columns. In one write your own views – not in prose but as bullet points. See the points are not repeated. In the second column write views of the other person. If possible, opposite your own relevant view. Then see how the two sides can compromise – in the process you become an unbiased umpire. After a while you will have the solution.

It is the best solution, if the other person does not accept the solution, that is their problem. Not quite, but then go for a compromise as best as you can.

However, out of love & relationship you may want to give up some of your rights/advantages. But that is as they say you are being more than fair in trying to come to an amicable solution.

How far back do you go to balance the equation? May be 1 year, 2 years, 10 years. Decide before starting the analysis.

You have to be on the dance floor first for Lady Luck to dance with you.

When you take a tough step forward, it seems the whole universe conspires to help you move forward and succeed.

It is really a way of saying that once you decide to move forward and take on a tough job, you are so focused that you find ways to succeed. You will explore various alternatives to find solutions to get over the obstacles, talk to whoever you can find you think can even remotely help, you will see so many coincidences that it feels surreal - that where were all these opportunities hiding.

My favourite One Liner is *"You have to be on the dance floor first for lady luck to dance with you"*.

Chance favours only the prepared mind.

- Louis Pasteur

Only when I am fully immersed in a task does my mind spot that here is something that will take my task forward.

Value of Technology and financial Investment in starting a business is high. Soon after starting the marketing becomes the most important function.

Technology and shareholding are totally unrelated.

Technology developers get paid, and the technology belongs to the company. Investors who take risk with their money buy shares in the company and reap benefit as dividend or share value appreciation.

In the initial stages I put marketing on the back burner, for I cannot fight alone on all the fronts, so I decided to make a perfect (first time in India) product which will have no difficulty selling, if it was perfect. But soon after the competition looms large over your head and the need for marketing.

You will win when no stakeholder in the transaction loses.

While this apparently is truer for business ethics and principles it is equally applicable in normal life as well! **Manas** (founded 1982) followed the principle from day one. We will be more than fair to our customers, suppliers, and employees. However, some of them will never be satisfied and will keep whining. But that is their problem.

A clear conscience is the softest pillow to sleep on at the end of a busy day.

I Promise.

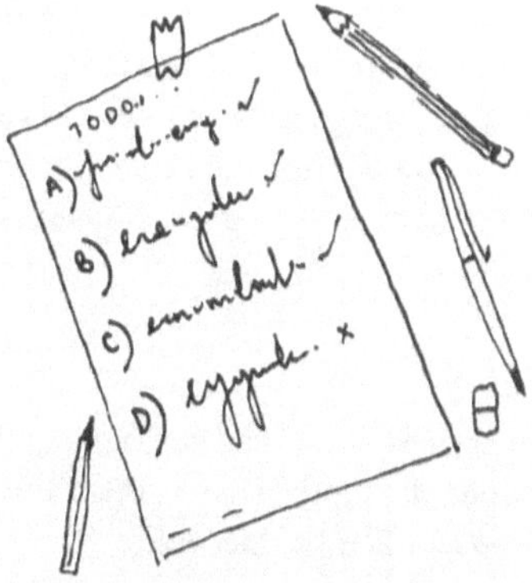

It is a small two-word phrase and perhaps the most devalued. Do not devalue the phrase. Take special care.

Around 1982 when I started Manas, I formally put down in company guidelines what was my definition of a 'Promise'. I find it has stood the test of time. Here is what I said then:

The statement you make does not have to have the word promise in it. The way you put across the words will lead the other person to assume it to be a promise. For example, I will be there at 4 PM to pick you up and I do not reach there until then. I have broken a promise. Specially making a junior wait is just not done. They will never tell you of the discomfort suffered by them. There are other unsaid promises, for example, to review employees' salary on time, paying their salaries on time. Providing help in times of emergency. Keeping your work area safe.

You negotiate a price to sell your products. And when the time comes you discover someone else is willing to buy it at a higher price. You renege on the contract. This is not done. You have broken a promise.

You promise to take your family out for the evening. At the last moment, you cancel this in favour of some work at office/factory. Not acceptable.

However, with changing times the phrase, "I promise", is getting devalued by the day and is used casually.

I stand by the classic definition of 'Promise' and it has stood me in good stead and given me confidence that I have not let anyone down. It is a two-way transaction. Once people know you, your work becomes easier. I could trust them that an honest and best effort will be made.

Some other examples:

Tripti my wife, in her last years was having cognitive decline. She was afraid to be alone. I simply promised that I will not leave you alone. I will be around when you need me.

One day (October 16, 2020) she called out from the bathroom, *"I need help, I can't locate the tap"*. I went in and helped. I like to believe that if you have the intention then all the forces in nature tend to come together to help. This was the first time in 55+ years of our being together that she really called out for simple help, it is only providence that I was around there and heard her voice.

The next day she seemed to be in good spirits and I persuaded her to come along and go for fitting a hearing aid that could improve her quality of life a bit. At other times like she got hurt while out on a walk. But that was different, she would bear the pain until she got back home. Tripti was an epitome of ability to bear pain.

She passed away the next day in sleep. Her laboured breathing woke me up in the night. About 10 breaths later she was gone. Providence helped me keep my promise.

In fact, I believe once you make genuine effort to keep your promise, all the forces in the world seem to come together to help you keep your promise. Try, it works. You even get a premonition whether you will be able to keep your promise. I have experienced it again and again.

Give someone a small gift or a hand-written note for a good deed they have done to you.

I am not good at it. But Tripti was. Give someone a present when they least expect it. I manage to find an occasion once in a while. I have sometimes written a thank you note. But I keep trying.

Isaac, my boss in England at ICI, one morning walked up to me and presented me a packet of Darjeeling Tea. Because, the previous week he was talking about how we were settling down in England and I remarked – I just can't find good tea here. In retrospect we were so new that we had not tried special shops beyond large supermarkets. But it was a gesture that left a permanent mark on my memory.

Give someone a small gift or a hand written note for a good deed they have done for you. Does not matter, even if it is in the course of regular work. It will make your as well as the recipient's day.

Training of the mind (TOM).

TOM is a better word than meditation.

During the last 30-40 years (I am 62 now), I have heard a lot about meditation and what it can do. Opportunity provided by FUR (Dalai Lama Foundation for Universal Responsibility) was great introduction to the TOM. This is one benefit I would have missed if I was not a member of IHC. And I might not have known that it was there. I have practised *yogasans* off and on since 1970 and more diligently since about 2005. I have read a fair bit about 'living'. The better living. I have my own beliefs. Some of them could be 'borrowed' simply because man has lived on this earth for ages and I read a lot over the last 50 years. Less so during the last few years.

Do not spend your time on the low-level choices. Save time!

An abundance of choices eats up a lot of my time. Try not to spend your time on the low-level choices. Does it matter what colour your toothbrush handle is?

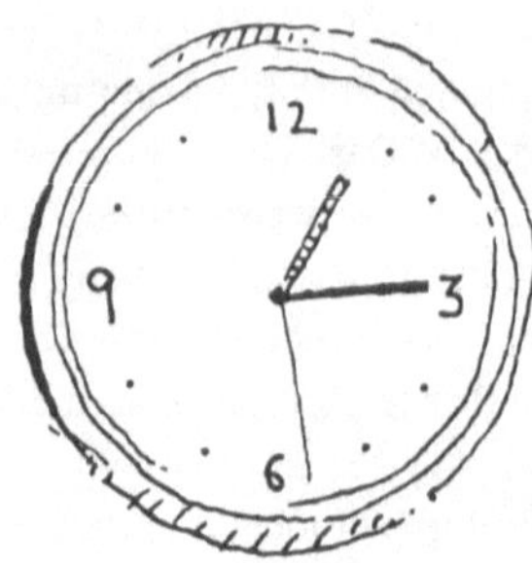

I 'automated' a lot of day's schedules. I limited my choices for tea or coffee. Such decisions would save a lot of time but once in a while I would enjoy walking through a big supermarket without buying anything. Or take the advice of a stores helper who is only interested in helping you and not pushing sales of anyone brand.

Idea crystallised after reading an article on 'breathingspace.com' in 2009.

Hiring a driver (since 1986) has turned my car rides into a great source of learning, thinking and knowledge gathering opportunity. I am careful that I do not fritter away this time into uncontrolled screen time or simply telephone chats. Only when I am in a new area do I consciously look outside the window to get to know the locality.

Time management is one of the well-researched activities with dozens of books around. You devise your own strategy depending upon what most suits you. I always have a book on the rear seat of my car for times that I am being driven. I open the book rather than curse the traffic.

To live a minimalist life, at odds with the life that
people live all around you is tough. In the early years
with limited availability of discretionary money
availability I was sure that we were not living a
resource wasting lifestyle.

By the time I had more money than what we needed
for a fair lifestyle, mid-eighties, my concern for
environment was higher and I made sure that for our
personal needs Tripti and I spent the bare minimum
but, in all ways, lived a comfortable life including
one or two holidays a year. Sometimes even a third
one. We even made it to UK on our 50th wedding
anniversary with children and grandchildren. Tripti
was mighty pleased. I am glad for her that we could
make it.

Anu gave me **Green Humour for the Greying
Planet by Rohan Chakraborty** one day in
September 2021, I leafed through it but found time
to seriously look at and read it today, Jauary 7, 2022.
Until now I was so overwhelmed by all the things,
I had to finish…this book explains a lot of what I
have felt for the past 30+ years about my living.
So, my awareness about the environment suddenly
improved a lot.

Do not have strong likes and dislikes.
My belief.

Then the word Hate will slowly disappear from your vocabulary.

Don't wish it were easier.
Wish you were better.

- Jim Rohn

For me every such occasion is a challenge to conquer.

And a source of small wins which when added up are a reason for celebration.

Do not waste your time on comparing yourself with anyone else.

Sometimes you will be ahead and at other times behind. The race is long, so compete with yourself. Just aim to do a bit better than what you were yesterday.

Look at and examine in detail the worst-case scenario of the decision you are about to take.

Then put this analysis behind you and embark on your journey.

Leaving a job and starting a business, what is it like?

No, you don't just leave a job one day and start your business the next day. It has to be a very thoroughly considered decision. I have no right to play with others' lives. I don't remember how much of the worst-case scenarios I have explained to Tripti but definitely nothing to my children Samit (11 years at that time) and Anu (8 years).

I was personally very clear that if all the efforts failed, I have the car and will run a taxi, with a service of the highest quality.

Stumble at times —
But get up and keep walking again.

It is the tenacity of purpose. Do not give up.

Rome was not built in a day.

Get small wins, celebrate.

I am constantly on the lookout for tips and tricks
to improve upon my current practices. If there is
no one else, then I just celebrate by myself and
continue cycling on the route for more innovations or
whatever is currently my chosen field of work.

How do you celebrate alone – write me a mail!
I am always there. E-mail address in preface.

Small wins give you courage to keep moving.

A mountaineer gets to the summit one step at a time. I am not one but, I once joined the Delhi Mountaineering Club for a hike in Solang Valley, around 1998. All the hikers were divided in small groups. Our team leader had been on such hikes before. The distance would be covered in about an hours' walk. The guide gave clear directions to all team leaders. They had been in the area before. Our leader took the usual route. He had not come the previous year. When a new easier shortcut had been discovered. We continued upstream of the Beas on its right bank.

Slowly small rocks turned into large boulders with sharp edges and sloping on both sides. I was a novice. There was no going back. Others of our team were ahead of me. I had to catch up. The 'Hunter' rubber soled shoes were great for walking on these stone wedges. Only way I could see was an occasional glance ahead for general sizing up of situation and then my shoes. I estimated the length of each jump/hop. There were encouraging words from people ahead.

I caught up and they were waiting for me to arrive. I did. One hop, step and jump at a time.

As soon as I caught up, the team started to climb the next section. They did not realise that I needed a break. Next it was a grassy slope to climb. Very slippery due to previous night's rain. There was only one way, up the slope. We could see all the other teams up there, having reached there by the new route. The short climb of 100-150 steps was treacherous. My other companions in the team got to the road in minutes. I took may be 20-30 minutes. Each step up precisely measured and heel dug into slippery grass. I was sweating profusely in a cold weather. But I could not risk my balance while trying to take off my sweater. There were shouts encouraging me. But all I saw was the foot hold for my next step. There was no time to stop and stare at the beautiful frothy Beas flowing below.

Finally, I joined the team. Once there, I looked down at the gorgeous Beas flowing. I would not go on that route again. But it clearly reminded me. Small wins – one step at a time – gave me the courage to continue.

Years later as business continued to grow, I have experienced it multiple times – small wins gave me courage to keep going forward.

Look for small wins   OL 51
and these together will
make a great past to look
upon and cherish.

Day started as usual. The following is a record of what happened.

Slept early. The previous night with stomach 75% full. Woke up very early and did some reading, soaked clothes for washing No waking up for bathroom visit at night. Taught Hukam English. Finished my usual session of Yoga. These are just 'small wins' and these can make a day great! (See OL 133)

Indira Nooyi said –
"Don't feel like that you have to do all, but always be in a position to fend for yourself"

Very simply, there is not enough time in life to do all you may want to do. So be prepared to curtail your ambitions.

In effect you have to become good at 'triaging'. And then a step ahead to have the courage to discard some projects.

Need Vs. Want Vs. Desire.

I had a long list of desires.

My gurus said desires and wants are to be controlled if I wanted to attain success in life. But I believed suppressing a desire causes more unrest in mind. For an uninitiated human I believed, giving in to desires so that my mind is at rest for other essential tasks rather than a conflict which does not allow me to chase my dreams.

So, what I did was to set a time/money limit to fulfil my desires. If I could not achieve those within these limits then I applied my ever-handy principle: ***"If you cheat yourself then even the God can't help you".***

I therefore, trained myself mentally – auto suggestions – , through *Yog Nidra* to say that is the limit and no further. I found a book ***'Yog Nidra'*** by Swami Satyanand Saraswati as a good introduction to the subject. It is a powerful technique and starting lessons need only 12 –15 min. each once a day.

Ask an unstructured question
and you could get interesting answer.

To keep the conversation going and make it interesting, ask a
question on an unrelated topic. For example: what does your mother
do? Most times (in India at least) you will get a blank expression on a
young person's face!

But you could steer the conversation with generalizations like I know
of no woman who has not done something specific and interesting for
her kids. Be prepared to talk about what your mother did?

I once asked a friend of mine what his father does? I learnt he was a
professor in philosophy before he recently retired. Going further
I learnt that this friend of mine himself was well read in the subject.

Or you can ask an innocuous one like – *"What do you think of the
upcoming elections?"*

Or make a self-deprecating statement.

Call a spade a spade.

Not easy. I therefore, have less friends around than so many other
people I know of.

Hypocrisy allows you to be seen as a nice person in the short term.
While it hurts others at the same time. But it comes back to haunt
oneself in the longer term. While I may be seen as a nice person.
I strongly believe that there is nothing to be gained by being a
hypocrite. The person opposite behaves nicely simply because
they do not want to be seen as unsocial. If you do not give honest
feedback, you are letting the other person go to harm. Is that ok? Not
by my way. I would rather caution the person opposite than be seen
as a nice person. I am at peace that I cautioned the other person.

Leave every place a little better than how you found it, when you came there.

I am a visitor at any place I go to. It is a bit philosophical. Any way.

Most of the time these are places I own or share with immediate family – for example, kitchen, bedroom, office desk, verandah I was relaxing in, the lab I went in for a small experiment and so on.

If I did not follow this one liner, there is no way I can insist on others to follow the principle. I do not want to be clearing up the mess others created. I have no time. Nobody has the time. So, everyone needs to clean up and not leave a mess for someone else to clean. Yes, you may have a household help or a lab helper to do the clean-up. But it is my job to see that the clean-up has been done. I cannot get away by saying *"I told him/her to do the clean-up"*. And he/ she did not do it. If I gave the instructions for something to be done and I am seeing it is done, then at the same time I need to give an instruction to clean up when the job is done. And it is my job to see that the second instruction (to clean up) is also followed. Soon a stage will come when anyone who comes to work there will find it inviting to work.

Let this be the axiom for your workplace and you insist that all users respect it. Or else it will be a mess and one day, no one will be able to work there in peace.

When you get fed up of being fed up, you will change.

The quote gave me the confidence that I can do it. Nothing is beyond us.

As an example, I further decided to once in a while spend one hour a day for a few days sorting out the accumulated papers. It took me about 10-12 one-hour session to sort out the mess. And I had carried this heavy strain on my mind for many long years!

If you cheat yourself or lie to yourself, not even God can help.

If I cheat myself, I have only downhill to go.
For example, I cannot go for a walk because I have
lack of time in the morning. I cannot read in the
evening because I am always tired at the end of
the day and so on. Well, I need to create time in
mornings. Or find time to read when I am not tired.
The decision is clearly mine on what I want out of
those 24 hrs.

I was standing next to a friend who is cleaning his
car. Small talk ensued. At one point I proffered my
advice: I think you should consider some regular
workout. Pat came the answer: car cleaning is my
workout also. I was dumbfounded.

Stop cheating myself (yourself).

A variation on the above. Not doing something I said
I would do. For example, clean/tidy my desk before
winding up for the day. Am I trying to cheat myself?
Who am I trying to fool? Someone who does not
know my inside? No, it is me. Someone who knows
'me' inside out. So, stop cheating myself (yourself).
If you mean business seriously, you will not cheat
yourself, much less anyone else. After all honesty has
to be the hallmark of my business. I have restarted
doing this some time back. And it has helped me a
lot. Such occasional introspection acts as a reprimand
to myself. Chastises me. It is my teacher.

Trust but verify. Can you put a hand on your heart and say.........?

Can you put a hand on your heart and say I have been honest? That is my way of arousing someone's conscience one more time before they knowingly dump their ethics for short term gain.

There are times when someone feels they can get away by a minor cheating in a deal. But in any transaction there is always only one honest path. So I need to remind the person concerned that they have made a mistake. It is done such that the person opposite can withdraw honourably from their wrong doing before the point of no return.

Keep my eyes and ears open. चलता है, नही चलेगा!!!

(English equivalent — quick fix, a temporary solution, make shift solution)

This is a classic Indian habit on the shop floor. I tried to put a stop to it at my work place. It makes the whole environment safer – e.g., no poorly insulated electrical connections.

It applies not just in a factory but equally in the home. It is a habit that must be discouraged.

There is no better way to catch an opportunity. And in a laboratory no better way to maintain safety.

I want to be my own boss.

It is easier said than done.

If you are even a bit serious about the statement
above, then you will need to sit down with a pen and
paper to do an analysis to see pros and cons of being
your own boss.

I did such thinking analysis many times before I took
the plunge and quit the well-paying job to start on my
journey into the hazy future. To clear the haze and
find the sun and deflate a bloated ego that needed to
be controlled with ruthless self-restraint. See details
in - **How did I start my business?** In an adjunct to
this book.

The dilemmas were many. Social and personal. For
example, If I fail it will substantially impact Tripti
and children's life; a failure would mean a social and
professional stigma for life – 1980s were not the days
of Start-ups.

The next job will be difficult to come. Can you trust
this man who has failed?

Will not take a revenge any more than the damage the other person has caused.

I could try and extract more. I may even succeed at
times. But it is in bad taste. I know the other party
will not sit quietly and strike back at the earliest
opportunity.

बदला नहीं — no revenge OL 64

The view crystallised sometimes in the last ten years or so (2005-2010). After I realised that there is no way you can undo what someone has done unto you.

As a principle in my business, we are more than fair to our opponent.

A business or a relationship does not grow by a one-time small benefit. I shall never look for revenge or for an opportunity to level out for what I thought was an injustice done to me.

It has been tough trying to follow this principle. But the effort made to follow this has brought its own rewards. For one, the mind is at peace because whatever had to happen has happened and I can move on in life. If I react/retaliate with an equal force, so will the other person. And there will be no end to a fight.

However, sometimes I have had to take up the fight in a court of law against what I consider is a totally unjust situation. And we have won there, simply because we gave the other side too much leeway that they were just too much at fault when we finally went to court.

Over a period, we have accumulated enough instances that the other party knows we are more than fair.

A wonderful little book on the subject is ***"Winners Never Cheat"*** by Huntsman. It should be an essential reading for all people in business.

Am I afraid of God? For what it might do to me or might it curse me.

Yes, absolutely. No two ways about it. It might seem incongruous to those who know me well.
I do not believe in God, but I pretend to when I am in the company of lesser known people or I do not know very well. This is simply to make life easier. Otherwise, there will be too many coffee table conversations and time wasted.

God to me is a 'being' beyond humankind to whom I can attribute all situations that I fail to resolve and move on in life.

Get to know your parents; you never know when they would be gone for good.

When his father was in India, he one day asked from US, what was his favourite car, the dad said *"I really wished I had a red Merc"*.

'Why didn't you tell me about it all this time.' Chef Khanna said. The father replied *"but you never asked me even once"* and he was gone before his next visit to India!

In retrospect I did not know my parents well, until I started looking at some old accumulated papers he had left behind, to incorporate some of those ideas while writing this book.

The myth of quality time.

It is as if you can programme yourself and the other person to find quality time at the same instant. Real bonding happens instantly – unplanned. You cannot say *"this evening I will spend one hour of quality time with my cousin"*. Quality time to me is when I can walk into my friend's home unannounced or with minimal prelude to the visit and have a chat.

I only discover time spent was quality time after the event. Using such phrases would make it easier for me to cheat myself. Sometimes you could simply be with a friend or relation without talking much or doing anything and the experience can be exhilarating. You need spontaneity in the moment.

In the real world I need to inform the other party when I am coming to meet them, after all I would not want to drive for an hour and a half and find that their home is locked because they had gone to meet some of their friends.

Respect your elders.

At some stage of your growing up you think/believe you know more than these old people around.

My father once told me when I was about 20 and we differed vastly on some point that we were discussing. He said *"the young think knowledge is everything (which they have a lot) and the old think that experience is all that matters, but know that the truth lies somewhere in between."* I saw his point and the argument was over!

Being a parent is tough.

Children have no patience. They do not want to be
judged. But how do you tell them that they could be
wrong?

When things do not get accepted, I am part of a
scared tribe called parents.

I quietly in private allow those tears to flow and
frustration to scream because these are the only
things that will heal me.

Advice is a form of nostalgia, trying to do through your children, what you could not do yourself.

Don't control their lives. Let them live theirs as you
have liked to live your own. That is how the world
will be different.

My advice is probably worth much less than what
I think. I realised it as years went by.

Don't be reckless with other people's heart.

"Do not be reckless with other people's heart.

Do not put up with people who are reckless with yours"

From - Everybody is free to wear sunscreen
(Lee Perry)

I love this quote.

"Breaking the rules.
Do unto others as you would have
them do unto you"

- Aesop's fables.

I shall not be the first one to break the rules. I will not be the first to hurt a living being (this includes mental & physical hurt). I believe in Gita's axiom – do your duty (job, work) and do not expect a reward, fruit of the act if any will come on its own.

Underprivileged need support. They could be economically weak or in India – women. Keep your promise – always.

Do not give up if you believe a child needs to be protected from undesirable influence.

OL 74

You need to rein in children's behaviour at an early age. How much and how decides how your child will be different from you and other influencers in your family. I could see stark differences between me and Tripti's way of bringing up children.

Do not give up if you believe a child (your child) needs to be protected from undesirable influence. I would fight on principles with anyone.

It is better to have loved and lost than to have never loved at all.

OL 75

Some quotes / One Liners can communicate before they are understood. It is one of them, like OL 1 in this book.

छिमा बड़न को चाहिये, छोटन को उत्पात
कह गए संत कबीर

The young make mistakes, but elders need to pardon
/overlook those.

It is a great learning. While Kabir perhaps meant
kids but I interpret it as mistakes made by younger
(or inexperienced) people that I should ignore but
suitably guide them on to the right path.

Happiness or joy.
Be with people for life
rather than for your need.

As long as another person is involved it will never
happen the way you want it.

You should be joyful by yourself and not because of someone else.

Some notes from one of Sadhguru's talk:

a. You are joyful by yourself and not because something is happening or not happening outside of you.

b. Once you leave yourself in the hands of other people your being is a questionable thing.

c. You get used to many things and you think that is life.

You think the problem is your home/your job. If you get fired from the job and thrown out from home, will you be happy?

Suffering happens when you live the past or the future, so live in the moment.

Long term relationship needs tolerance.

My wife frequently lamented that one who has no love for music can even murder a person in cold blood. And my retort was for her to remain cautious!

Don't do anything today that you will be ashamed of 5, 10, 20 .... years later.

Tough, but I wish someone had told me this in my early life.

There is no way you can travel into your past to correct what you are ashamed of having done then. You will at times be in dilemma, especially when dealing with the opposite sex. It is best to seek the other person's concurrence. You may be discussing a colleague's actions, then err on the side of extreme caution. There is no way you could go back in time to undo what you may end up doing.

Retreat and take time to decide.

Character is doing the right thing when no one is watching!

Yes!

Do you throw that toffee wrapper out of the car window because no one is watching or no one can catch you?

Some valuable advice from my wife!

You value absence of something but not of one that is present. Try and value things while they are there. I valued Tripti while she was there but I see I miss her more often while she is no more.

Here are a few quotes from her which I value:

Walk straight, walk tall.

Sit straight

Walk a mile after dinner.

Trust but verify.

I like the phrase.

If you look up the meaning on the net, it gets confusing with all the history of how this phrase was introduced in the cold war era in nuclear negotiations between US and Russia.

However, I take it to mean start your negotiations with full faith in the opposite party. And as time goes on keep verifying your initial assumptions. Modify your views to the extent required.

So unequivocally I will want the other side to understand that we trust them. Nobody prevents you from changing your views midway, if you find trust lacking on the other side.

Make a promise and believe in it.

I have many cases where I made a promise and even when the environment changed it helped me keep my word.

Caveat: Don't be foolhardy and make just any promise. Think and then go ahead.

I have found that environment changes to help you keep your promise.

Adding life in my years

The bright Spark - why do I or anyone else aspire to live longer?

Not because I enjoy life or enjoy eating a biscuit with my morning tea but because I can create something and leave it for others to enjoy (Even without their knowing who created it) when they come face to face with it. Perhaps an anonymous gift.

Live each day as if it is your last day.

Do what you believe is great work and do what you love.

Keep looking, do not settle.

If you live each day as if it is your last, someday you will be right.
And in the earlier days you would have achieved so much that you
will move into the next world without saying *"I wish I had ...."*.

I have no experience in this regard! But have read so much that
I believe what I have said above.

Someone asked– what is forgiveness?

A little boy replied:

It is the wonderful fragrance that a flower gives as it is being
crushed.

How did these One Liners help me get to my destination?

An important source of my learning has been to go
and study a subject in depth when it is going to touch
my life substantially. Thus in 1991-93 I studied Laurie
Baker's low-cost brick building construction technique.
I ended up building my farm house using his technique.
I studied and practiced rat trap brick construction. I
would dabble in anything that involved innovation
or skills in different areas. I thus experienced: aero-
modelling, wood working, - manual and machinery like
lathes, planers, photographic developing and printing.
Those were the days of box cameras and dark rooms
for printing and developing. Crafts of various types –
leather, paper, papier mâché, sculpting and so on.

Mental growth

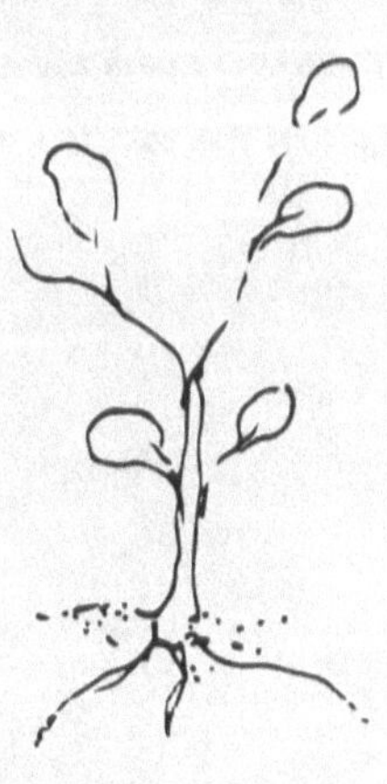

OL 88 Aim to be better than my parents in "acquired learning".

OL 89 If you don't use it, you lose it!

OL 90 Compete with yourself to go up the ladder of life.

OL 91 Do something that others cannot do or fear to do.

OL 92 Do not have strong likes and dislikes for food.

OL 93 Don't fall in love with any of your ideas, when short...

OL 94 How does one choose a challenge?

OL 95 Challenge yourself to finish a mundane task with perfection.

OL 96 Make fewer bets and then saturate them with resources.

OL 97 Problem solving. Define what you want in one short sentence.

OL 98 Have courage to follow your heart.

OL 99 Do your best, howsoever small your contribution be...

OL 100 Neither a borrower nor a lender be, for money loses both...

OL 101 There is no point in cramming up your mind with...

OL 102 I will pardon first act of injustice.

OL 103 If I have to pick up a fight the person has to be of a...

OL 104 Create more time for yourself. (Can time be created?)...

OL 105 Three principles by Swapan Seth.

OL 106 Books do not laugh at you!

OL 107 I am the product of the books I have read.

OL 108 Do one thing every day that scares you.

OL 109 Give back to the communities in some way.

OL 110 What you write and speak does not stop there, it goes 'in'...

OL 111 Make a note of a good day once in a while.

Aim to be better than my parents in "acquired learning". My own first One Liner

I coined this for myself when I was in school unaware that such a thinking would end up as a One Liner. It is a statement fraught with danger.

We have been taught – in Indian culture – not to question our parents and their wisdom. It may be true in your younger days. But at some stage you will grow up to be smarter than your parent(s). Still, you respect them for their wisdom and continue to surpass them in what I would term as acquired learning. That is the only way the world/ civilisation progresses.

Otherwise, won't we all still be living in caves as hunter gatherers? This spirit of competition propels humanity in progress but I would watch out that in this progress we do not toss ethics away!

If you don't use it, you lose it!

If you don't use it, you lose it! It is the principle that I have followed for decades. It includes physical ability as well as mental ability.

But it came into stark perspective once again with ***"My Story, Insult to Injury"*** by Kathryn Kuitenbrouwer in Reader's Digest of Jan 2013. A boy suffers PTSD (Post-traumatic stress disorder) and stops using certain limbs. His health is revived when non-use of limbs was discovered as a possible cause.

I started on muscle related exercise in my 81st year and amazed how much more flexibility I could achieve in all my joints within about a month. Why didn't I learn of such exercises earlier?

Compete with yourself to go up the ladder of life.

There is too much hypocrisy around. It is difficult to find honest advice or feedback these days. Every piece of advice is given with receiver's reaction (like/dislike) in mind.

There is no one – who will give you the honest advice that you can take as a yardstick. So, I judge myself against what I was yesterday. And it helps me go up the ladder of life.

Do something that others cannot do or fear to do.

Sunil Ghanekar – (February 5, at Plastindia) – has started a factory for manufacture of LED lights for street lighting. He said he did what I challenged them to do when we were at Cosmo.

In simple terms: Do not be scared of picking up challenges.

Do not have strong likes and dislikes for food.

I love food. I love eating. I overeat occasionally. But I am not a slave to my tongue. I can eat the same food day after day. Food is a means to an end and not an end in itself. I choose what I eat.

Contradictory? No that is the reality of life.

As my daughter once remarked, eat food like a dog. You give the dog the same food day after day, he still wags his tail.

I love the simile!

Don't fall in love with any of your ideas, when short listing your ideas.

This is one of the major hurdles that prevents
your achieving success in your initiative to start a
business of your own. Make sure that you have a
minimum of five ideas to explore for your start-up. If
you have only one idea you could easily get into one
of several traps.

E.g., You run short of cash. You borrow some more
and then some more. Now you are getting into a
situation where you will fail.

You need to choose your own limits for each
criterion, e.g., first review at x lakhs spending. Or
move on to the an alternate project after a total of
y lakhs spent without any return. Or I will discard
this project if I have no success after…months. The
point is to set your own limits. Do not cheat yourself.

How does one choose a challenge?

Mountaineer Todd Skinner provides a hint:

If you are not afraid, you have probably chosen too
easy a mountain. To be worth the expedition, it had
better be intimidating… A mountain well within your
ability is not only a misspending of resources, it is
a loss of opportunity across a lifetime of potential
achievement.

Challenge yourself to finish
a mundane task with perfection. OL 95

Mundane definition/meaning: Dull, lacking interest or excitement, tedious, something that is typical or ordinary, everyday routine.

It is very important for me that every so often I do a mundane task perfectly. It wakes me up to the need of doing a task with full concentration. It also tells me what the life is like on the other side and be more sensitive to my colleagues' lives.

It creates dignity of labour. I did, have great satisfaction of seeing some of my colleagues doing very well in life. However, I do remember that it will eat into some of my time. But it is a gift that only my time could give my associates. Money could not have done it, ever.

Make fewer bets and then
saturate them with resources. OL 96

It goes counter to my belief and practice that you must be working on several projects at a time. For you never know which one could face hurdles during development or research stage.

Once you can clearly see which one has a clear path forward then saturate that with resources. This is a good commercial strategy. It is simple to appreciate. If you have 5 projects going and after two years each of them is about 80% through then you (company) have no returns on investment. But even with one successful and four others only 70% done, you have income to support the others. After all business is there to make a profit for general growth of all concerned.

Problem solving.
Define what you want in one short sentence.

Define what you want in one short sentence. In broad terms but not too broad.

For example, I need fairly rigid/impervious/ waterproof/may not be solvent resistant/coating on granules.

………. And then look at all the possibilities.

Have courage to follow your heart.

"Have courage to follow your heart" – Steve Jobs

It is easier said than done!

Generally, whenever deciding between two alternatives money (cost/ profit/loss) will be involved. Look at these factors and then take a conscious decision.

Do your best, howsoever small your contribution be. It all adds up.

'Who will take charge of my work?',

Says the setting sun.

Hearing (this) the world keeps mum

Like a picture dumb.

An earthen lamp was there;

It said 'My Lord,

I shall strive to do the best I can'.

By **Rabindranath Tagore**

Neither a borrower nor a lender be, for money loses both itself and the friend.

I even include family in this quote. There are occasions when you feel the other person is in dire need and there is no option but to lend. I found a simple solution to this dilemma. Lend the money by all means but mentally write that off. If you get it back, you are richer!

Once I started following this principle, I had no mental strain that I have to get my money back and how do I ask for it. You do not, because it is no longer your money.

There is no point in cramming up your mind with information that can be found in a book.

There is no point in cramming up your mind with
information that can be found in a book (or today
on the net). I was never good at memorising for
examination at school or college level. I lost out
here. I believed that learning by rote what can be
found in a book is no great deal. So, I had mediocre
marks in exam all the time.

Development of thinking abilities stood me in good
stead when I got a job at ICI in England and when
I started my business in 1982.

I will pardon first act of injustice.

May be even second. But then I will hit back. This is
when the opposite party is equal or stronger than me.

For a person weaker than me, I would not hit
back. Weaker in any manner – stature, strength,
economically, or whatever. I would then try and see
if I can find any other way. It especially includes
women, who in Indian society have been the most
disadvantaged class. In fact, most people would say
I am partial to women folk.

If I have to pick up a fight the person has to be of a higher level than me.

No point fighting with a weaker person or a junior at work. Yes, I know many religions – including Jainism propagate a no revenge teaching. I do not have that much of patience. I am not that much of a saint – I live in a real world. In a rustic world I might consider forgiving for damage done to me but I cannot tolerate someone taking advantage of my being nice. I shall not be the first one to retaliate. Never. In real life, I will always overlook the first transgression on my rights. May be even second or third for some selected people and then distance myself from the person opposite me.

Create more time for yourself. (Can time be created?)...

A car is to take me from point A to point B.

To elaborate, last 40 years in addition to the above, the car allowed me an extra two hours a day of reading time because I had hired a driver, while I was commuting through crowded NCR roads. A driver does mean less discretionary money available for personal expenses but the driver also reduced my tension on the road!

Three principles by Swapan Seth.

Don't make a promise when you are in joy.

Don't reply when you are sad.

Don't take a decision when you are angry.

Books do not laugh at you! OL 106

You go to a book.

It never laughs at you; however ignorant may you be.

It is willing to share all it has.

I loved books, and still do.

I am the product of the books I have read. OL 107

One book is not the view point of one person. A good book offers you a panorama of many minds. If I am careful, I can look into all those beautiful minds.

Two authors that have made most impression on me have been Edward de Bono and Sadhguru Jaggi Vasudev.

Do one thing every day
that scares you.

Innumerable times I postponed action because I was scared of it
on various counts – Do I have the ability to do it? Will I meet the
standard required for the task in hand?

It would take too long to finish the task, so do it tomorrow or leave
it until the evening. Then it is too late and I would leave it for
tomorrow! It is too boring. May be tomorrow I will have more energy
to tackle the job. I have an endless list of excuses tucked away
somewhere.

Finally, one day it got done. What did I discover? This undone
task took away so much of mind space that it made me an expert at
finding excuses for why something could not be done. And above
all it delayed so many other tasks. So, for some time now, I decided
to do one job once in a while that has scared me for one reason or
another. I remember reading it at more than one place.

I discovered its value when I was stuck sorting out my investments.
These were made, because of my saving habit, in small amounts and
at different time. It kept piling up in pieces of papers, emails, hard-
copy mails of yesteryears.

All these papers got sorted out quickly when I applied the above
axiom.

Give back to the communities
in some way.

Contribute to the local charity or contribute in any other way for the
betterment of the community. I don't have to publicise but do my
little bit without singing about it.

An anonymously given donation (*gupt daan*) is the best you can do.

What you write and speak does not stop there, it goes 'in' ...

What you write and speak does not stop there, it goes 'in' and taints the soul or affects how you perceive and behave.

Make a note of a good day once in a while.

Make a note of a good day once in a while to remind you that your life has a pleasant side, too, which is easily forgotten when a not so good day appears.

Here was a day to remember yesterday **29-01-21**.
Everything went as per schedule I had made – leave home for farm between 10-11. Before that do two hours of work – office/farm. Downloaded Tripti's bank statements smoothly – internet banking always causes me mismatch in filling up forms. Read some stuff on internet. Finished bath and I was out for farm before 11. Bath was good relaxing.

At the farm again the usual going round the place. Then some work on computer - printing Tripti's bank statements. Finished dinner by 7:50 and went to bed at 8:30.

I also found some more info on breathlessness. This was also printed out. To top it all I didn't have to get up in the middle of the night until 1:45 for a bathroom visit. I hope this condition becomes a normal. Finally woke up at 3:15. Fresh to start another fine day.

30.1.21
It is 7:30 now and I think today could be better than yesterday with painting included after two hours of "office"/computer/writing work. Add to the above a general good health for last several weeks.

1-02-21
Another great day!

How did these One Liners help me get to my destination?

When I bought a 2-acre plot of farm land, my interests widened to include agriculture, horticulture, and all related areas (birds, soil, water, tube wells, life on countryside). This would reduce my attention to earlier interests. I allowed older ones like astronomy and telescope building to lapse.

Another major subject I studied was lateral thinking. I read and studied at least a dozen books by its proponent Dr De Bono. Most of my problem solving was done without any outside help, I was a one-man army.

Skilling and Learning

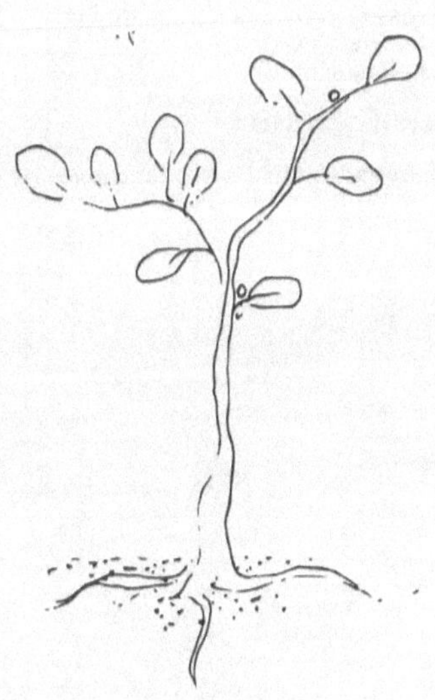

If it is a skill, it can be learnt.

Learn as many skills as you can. Skills are great to have in your quiver, especially if your specialisation is innovation in technology.

Innovation needs a very broad range of skills. After finishing school in 1958 I decided to learn anything that came my way (or my father could afford to pay for).

These included Carpentry, Cooking, Photography, working with leather, touch Typing (formal training in England at an evening school for typewriting the skill was to type correctly in first go. There was no 'del' key on mechanical typewriters. (A vocation considered suitable only for women at that time!), Glass blowing and many others.

Innovation Tricks.
It is simply hard work, but not a donkey's work.

Read, read, and read more to generate new ideas. And read books/articles in subjects that take off at a tangent to what your specialisation is.

Read at least two books a month. While you are young!

Opportunity to learn budgeting.
In fact, learn any skill beyond your routine.

With limited income it was imperative that expenses did not exceed salary my father brought home. When I was about 14 or 15, one day my father simply said – *"Here is the money for this month's household expenses and our allocation for various heads"*. He asked me if I could manage the expenses. I said yes. I meticulously kept the record. With 4-5 days for month to be over, all the money was finished. He looked at where the money went. And told me managing the expenses means not knowing where the money went but when you see that money is going where it was not planned for, then curtail expenses somewhere else.

a. I had learnt budgeting in one go!

b. Learn as many skills as you can.

Skills are great to have in your quiver. If your is innovation in technology learn various technologies to a fairly good level.

I also had the good luck that my father had faith in me at that early age.

Ask the right question!

For example, a colleague once sent out a query - *"I am looking for good quality polymers for spherical balls that can be blow moulded"*.

The reply came from the supplier after some days: *"Unfortunately we cannot comment on the suitability of TPX, our brand of the plastics, in your application as you have not mentioned the diameter of the ball and wall thickness"*.

However, supplier's data shows TPX is no use. Such an enquiry without even looking at supplier's data simply delays work. I would always make an effort to study a little of the background before embarking on queries to outsiders.

Chicken Test

I have always been in a terrible hurry to see the
result of my experiments/endeavour, so I would want
to test my ideas as fast as I could. My colleague at
ICI in UK in the 60s introduced me to the term Heath
Robinson setup.

We would use the term *Jugaad* in India. Tom Peters
used the term Chicken Test in his book, ***"In Search
of Excellence"***.

It does the wonderful magic of telling me whether
the idea is likely to work. If yes, then the project
needs more resources quickly. If not, do not give up
but put it on the back burner for a while. And I had
too many back burners at any given time!

Reframe the problem —
to innovate.

Go out into the world to experience.

When engaged in discussion to solve a problem
we tend to digress from the main issue. So, keep
reminding yourself of this fact and restate the issue
once in a while.

If I am given a problem to solve, I will first go and see where the problem is.

- Japanese Genchi Genbutsu.

No problem solving sitting at my desk.

Especially in a factory scenario I end up seeing more background than what was described to me as a problem.

Cut corners and success will be just that much more elusive.

In the course of development if you take a short cut by 1% a simple mathematical calculation will show you that within about 10 steps down you will be far away from a possibility of an accurate result. And when the product does not behave as you expected, you will never know which step is making that error.

I differentiate between two types of short-cuts. First are necessary to test a hypothesis quickly – to proceed further along a certain line of thinking and turn your thoughts into a permanent setup. The second are taken by certain people out of sheer laziness or couldn't care less attitude. The second type are to be avoided.

Maintaining focus.
Pause and recap.

I would pause frequently during a discussion, when led by me or I had a major say in that, with *"So ... to recap.... or let us just recap what was our aim/topic of discussion.... just to make sure we are not digressing from the target"*.

Compete against yourself.

Challenge yourself to do better than what you know you can. No one else needs to know it. You compete with yourself.

For example, peel mango faster perhaps whole peel in one piece, perhaps a long walk, shave off seconds or minutes from an activity to consistently get better/more efficient, seed the dates, skin potatoes.

All these come in handy when in factory. It allows me to develop concentration and skill, dexterity of fingers. It also makes me impatient when I see incompetence in others! Which I have to curb or teach the other person the skill.

Competing with others means I get into a rat race or begin to keep up with the Joneses. The competition with myself allows me to improve on any skill that I have or don't have.

For example, I got to start on water colour painting sometime in 2002. Then learning about trees in about 2008. There are innumerable such examples. It may even be a small project of how to make a perfect stuffed *paratha*. Or more recently target shooting.

It keeps creativity going and mind alert.

Do not use
present continuous tense.

This is what I try to do and impress upon the
youngsters joining to work with me, do too. I have
found frequently on further query that the task
remained undone. Yes, they are thinking about it and
no more details – like: how far they reached/are they
stuck somewhere/can I help …… couple of times
they shot back – don't try to micromanage me.

My retort is: How you manage yourself is your
business. I only want to know the status as of now
in past perfect tense or present perfect tense but not
in present continuous which in business tends to be
totally non- committal.

Jack of all trades and
master of ONE.

It is my play on words of the 1500's saying 'Jack of
all trades but master of none'.

As the complexity of vocations has increased, people
have had to specialize in their vocations but one
must remain competitive in their own specialization.
Hence the need to be a specialist while still
preserving the lead by being good in disparate fields.

Ideas are dime a dozen but have value, if you...

Ideas have value if you can translate any into a reality. Which means you prioritise them (that is invest more time and money). And then if you can find an investor to risk their money to take it to market and sell for a profit.

Or in the social context make life better. For example, Kailash Satyarthi's work with children. *'Samarth'* for Senior Citizens, *'Sewa'* for women and many others.

'Neem Hakim Khatrai Jaan'.

Literally it means "Beware of half-baked experts" or people who will proffer advice as if they were experts. How do you know that? Simple. Listen to your inner self. Finally, when you do take a decision, you can be sure it was your error of judgement and you will be better off next time.

The best part of it is that I stopped blaming others for my failures. With this my decision-making ability improved early in life.

There is always a better way of doing any job.

Look for alternatives, innovate. Be judicious. First find out what that way is and then proceed further. Or you may find the present one is adequate for your application. But do not accept what to you appears to be an inadequate solution.

Difference between being 99% right or 99.5% right.

As we try to cope with the advancing complexity of knowledge, we fall short in performance of even simple jobs. Openness in where we fail will drive improvement, if only, simply through embarrassment (I call it '*chintan*').

I do a job 99% right or 99.5% right. Does it make a difference? Not much or hardly. But when I add up the two performances slip consistently over a year the effect accumulates and one performance may be 80% while the other near perfect.

The two above are many of the gems from a book *'Better'* **by Atul Gawande**, a surgeon.

Do a repetitive job better than how you did it last time.

I practiced it ever since I started working. However, in recent years Atul Gawande's books have reinforced my belief in this axiom ever more. Doing it better every time means ultimately it kind of becomes an automated action. My errors in my experiments are less or nil. Results more trustworthy. Effort required is less. Drudgery of repetition is reduced. It leaves my time and mind free to work on more demanding tasks.

In any business there is always a hierarchy of people. I can expect to get excellence only if everyone works at their finest level. And it starts with me.

There are umpteen repetitive jobs being done all around. Just stop for a moment and see what life would be like if each of your *chapatti* was a polygon of a different number of side or your fresh lime soda came with different levels of sugar and salt.

An automation in a way leaves me with more free mind space to think of innovation. It cuts down effort in second and subsequent instances. Do better in all walks of life and work. However,

a. Be judicious. A 100% perfection may not be necessary all the time. Use your judgement. But a repetitive job needs to reach perfection.

b. It would need less effort as time goes on and you may even be able to pass it on to a less skilled person and save your time (after all a day has no more than 24 hours).

So how do you get better?

Quote from Atul Gawande's book:

The traditional view is you go to school, you study, you graduate and then you go into the world and make your way on your own. A professional is someone capable of managing their own performance.

The contrasting view comes out of the sports. They say you are never done; everybody needs a coach. Everyone. The greatest in the world needs a coach. Expert means not needing to be coached. Then you reach a limit and you do not know. You remain an expert, with knowledge stagnant, until you realise and you get a coach. "A coach is your external eyes and ears".

I did not like being observed. At times I did not want to have to work on things. I also felt there were periods when I would get worse before I got better. But it made me realise that coaches were on to something profoundly important". One of the fundamentally important matters is – communications.

Getting the nurses (juniors) to practice speaking up when something is wrong. When the baby mask is broken, or the gloves are not in stock or someone is not washing their hands. And then getting the seniors (managers) to practice listening. The result is "Anshikha". It means beautiful and she is what is possible when we really understand how people get better at what they do.

Another way of looking at it is: Anything that needs to be done repetitively needs to be done well.

Do find a good library, even if you must travel some distance to reach it.

The years I grew up (1954-1963 and for some time beyond that) there was no internet. Printed word was the prime source of learning. So, am I biased towards books as source of learning?

Not at all, I cannot live without internet. But books have their own place in life. Try reading a few books.

A teacher cannot refuse to help a student.

Remember Tulsi's couplet? The essence is like this:

One-day God and Guru appeared before me at the same moment.

Who do I greet first?

Tulsi thought about it and concluded –

"I greet the Guru first for it was the guru who taught me who/what a God is".

Empower young people.

Let them know you trust them to do a good job.
Mentoring is a prime job and responsibility of the
experienced and wise people, if not them (and you)
then who else?

The ultimate in perfection.

Javed Akhtar got this advice when he was small
(about 10 years) from a friend (Farooqui) of his
father. Become a grass cutter, if you like, but become
such an expert that if the top most person in the
world wanted to have his lawn mowed then it is you
who he would look for – On AIR FM Gold morning
time 7.8.2012.

Do something in life
that is not for money or
any material returns.

Know the joy and fulfilment of offering something that touches somebody's life forever.

I first experienced this when I was in class 6 (1951).

India had won independence a few years back and there was a lot of enthusiasm all around to do something or the other for the country. Our school initiated a programme to teach basic arithmetic and Hindi, reading and writing. We were given instructions on how to go about it. I chose to go to a *dhobi* ghat where our *dhobi* worked. Classes were held in the evening and it was one on one or two students to a teacher. We were around 10 years of age and our students from 20 to 50 years of age.

A few weeks later I asked them how they liked the class and if it was any use? Pat came the reply. *Saheb*, it has been very useful. How? Well, earlier *memsahib* will pretend to count the number of clothes and pay for the counted pieces washed and ironed. Last week when she counted the pieces, we said you made a mistake, there are more clothes than you counted and demanded the correct amount. The customer was taken aback and had no choice but to re-count and pay up the balance. The *dhobi* was ever grateful to us.

Hence, I say *"Give someone something that money cannot buy"*. Help them improve their life.

Since starting my own business in 1982, I have always offered to teach my employees English. I discovered while in school they passed the exams and gleefully claimed to have learnt English. But that knowledge was woefully inadequate. The few who learnt have been ever grateful to me since they got promotion and better recognition in their job.

How did these One Liners help me get to my destination?

All along my life my urge to start a business was in the
background with various ideas churning in the mind.

By 1982, time had come to take the plunge. With two
small kids in the family, it was a very considered risk that
I took to start a business. I started small in a *barsati* with
a capital of Rs. 5000/-, the first piece of equipment
I invested in was a laboratory oven.

This is how I founded my business and the story starts.
In the initial years I was always working on multiple
products. So, failure in one simply meant I switched to
other area while failure causes were sorted out or even
the product/that line of work abandoned.

Health and Retirement

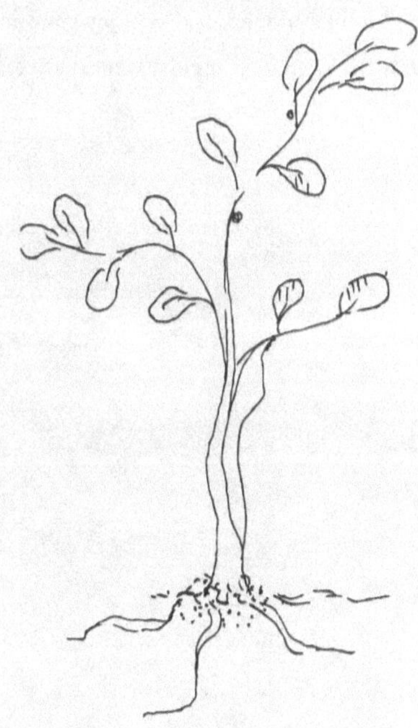

OL 135 Small actions/steps add up to a big treasure.

OL 136 Don't lose track of your living!

OL 137 My occasional notes tell me how I am progressing in life.

OL 138 Quick and Dirty Analysis – a good way of getting to a decision.

OL 139 If winter comes, can spring be far behind?

OL 140 Do not let yesterday take up too much of your today.

OL 141 Keep Fit. Good health cannot be compromised.

OL 142 Walk barefoot as much as possible.

OL 143 Life is not about waiting for the storm to pass it is about...

OL 144 One needs to have one's own standards.

OL 145 Keep Dancing through obstacles.

OL 146 Hug and peck are just too superficial.

OL 147 Do not live in the past but remember the future is built upon...

OL 148 Competition gives valuable adrenaline rush.

OL 149 I Counted my blessings, when I was young and do so now...

OL 150 Work until the last day of your life.

OL 151 Eat a little less at previous meal to enjoy your next meal.

OL 152 Keep Learning. Keep your inquisitiveness alive.

OL 153 Obituary!!

Small actions/steps add up to a big treasure.

Walk barefoot as much as possible. The heel works like a pump and assists blood flow.

Just stop and reflect on good times once in a while. It lifts the spirit and relaxes.

Stand and stare for a while if you happen to be amidst nature. It is such a busy life that unless you make it a conscious habit you will find no time to relax.

Make an unscheduled diversion to your daily commuting route and you might just see something unusual, in any case such a diversion is great for the brain as an exercise.

Don't lose track of your living!

The whole book is about living but this one refers to an important lesson for health that I learnt. Last food intake ideally should be at least two hours before bed.

My occasional notes tell me how I am progressing in life.

After Manas was established and I began to look out
how it could be made into a big business: something
like tens of crores turnover (in mid 90s). this meant
that I always had a very large to-do list so I was
struggling with apportioning time between health
maintenance, reading for personal improvement,
studying to innovate for new products, problem
solving in business and on personal fronts.

I was getting forgetful in 2007/2008 (age 66-67).
Examples, December 2007, dropped camera from car
at Barcelona 10-05-08. Forgot key in keyhole after
opening car door. Anu found it later.

Even checklist did not work sometimes. Example,
forgot jacket at home when I went to Pune in winter.
I guess status today (2021) is about the same. So, no
drop in cognition abilities (it makes me feel better!).
However, I know for sure that my energy levels are
lower. I take longer to finish a job and also take
longer to get started on a new job.

Scanning some older papers clearly showed that my
drop in thinking (and inefficiencies) had taken root
by about 2005-06. I am not able to shake out those
even today (November 2022).

Re-reading those notes gave me immense happiness
that my consistent writing had supported age related
deep decline in health.

Quick and Dirty Analysis —
a good way of getting to a decision.

I saw a tablet with Diya and then with Tarini.
I thought it could be a great help for me to do all my
pending jobs faster.

Then I stopped to think. Will it really or is it just my
imagination?

Here is an analysis and what I found hit me hard.

Why the tablet? What will it do for me?

- Typing easier with big keyboard.

- Painting possible – I should first learn it on paper.

- Its functions – varied.

- But what will it enhance for me? With age arrest
  declining Productivity?

- Where do I need productivity?

  I need Concentration/focus and getting rid of
  procrastination!

- Will allow me faster access on net (speed) – I am
  stuck with my age – ageing faculties.

- None of its features create more time or
  multitasking ability or create any of the above.

So, what do I need – maintain my faculties and get
rid of procrastination/do not vacillate/take minor
decisions quickly/avoid ducking the issues and
indecisions.

This simple analysis settled the issue even before
I came to price. I have done short, quick and dirty
analysis umpteen times to great advantage.

If winter comes, can spring be far behind?

Is a quote from PB Shelly 1792-1822. So, he lived for 30 years only! Titiksha quoted the crow and the pebble story to stress that we should not give up in adversity. I could not agree more.

So, I am making efforts to not fall in a trap of despondency since Tripti passed away in 2020.
I have included at least 15-20-minute walk in the sun (on colder days) to keep myself active. Further the schedule must include giving away something intangible every day.

"Do not let yesterday take up too much of your today"

- *Will Roger.*

One that needs no comments!!

Keep Fit. Good health cannot be compromised.

It is not in my hands not to fall sick. What if I caught Covid?

But what is in my control is most of my life.
Non-Covid time. And exercises or *Yogasans* to keep fit!

It is certainly possible to take precautionary measures
to maintain good health. I started on yoga in early 70s.
Perhaps my father's belief in yoga in some ways got
me into it. Now after a period of 50+ years of trying
to maintain good health I find that with Internet it is
up to an individual to ensure good health. Virtues of
good health have been enumerated so often in media,
both print and social that there is no point summarising
the same once again. I believe today I am able to
do physical and mental work several hours a day all
because of yoga and other exercises. A great dividend
from this attention paid to health maintenance.

Walk barefoot as much as possible.

Be as close to earth as practicable. No *chappals* inside
the home or a park. It is good for the heart and the
mind. Feel the grass, feel the mud and the nature.

"Life is not about waiting
for the storm to pass
it is about learning to dance
in the rain"

- Vivian Greene.

One needs to have one's own standards.

OL 144

S. Mannar Mannan - (February 5, Plastindia2020) –
Only last week I remembered you (DJ).

I told a friend just three days back that you had told
me this: An old man was walking with his little
grandson when on seeing a woman come from the
opposite direction, he lifted his hat and greeted her.
The little boy was surprised and asked his granddad
*"surely you know that the woman lacks virtue and
is talk of the town?"* Old man replied *"My dear
son, I greet a woman not because of what she is but
because I am a gentleman"*.

Keep Dancing through obstacles.

OL 145

I get up,

I walk,

I fall down,

Meanwhile I keep dancing

- Daniel Hillel

Hug and peck are just too superficial.

G.K. Gandhi in *'Of a Certain Age'*, about Kamla Devi Chattopadhyay – "Few very few in the shallow gaggles of the New Delhi of 1960s, 70s and 80s would dare try with her the meaningless hug and peck so characteristic of its superficiality."

It was true then and it is true now.

There are many other such social etiquettes that I needed to be aware of and get over them.

Do not live in the past but remember the future is built upon the past.

I started taking care of the future when I was around 60 years of age. But generally, around 50 when I read the first book on ageing.

Competition gives valuable adrenaline rush.

Celebrate your wins! Why can't you invite yourself for lunch (for one)?

Why does someone have to get a chocolate for you? Get one to celebrate your small wins.

I Counted my blessings, when I was young and do so now too when I am old.

I do that once in a while (by writing down). Here is one such recent list at 78!

1. I am not in pain or sick otherwise.

2. I maintain my exercise regime.

3. I have several friends and relatives whom I can visit and spend interesting hours.

4. I have the comfort of being at home.

5. I have the time to read and relax.

6. I have the time and good health to be able to go sightseeing alone.

Work until the last day of your life. OL 150

Retirement (no work situation) is a major cause of
health problems.

Be meaningfully engaged. Look for organisations
helping seniors find activities that will keep them
occupied.

Eat a little less at previous meal to enjoy your next meal. OL 151

An absolute truth!

Keep Learning .
Keep your inquisitiveness alive.

I Wonder Why?

Everyone speaks, I wonder why,

Let us find out let us try,

There are stories to tell,

And can be told really well,

Happy ones and sad ones.

Some really funny ones.

We also sing songs,

You can also sing along,

They help us to express,

Whether we are happy or in distress.

Then there is the speech,

To spread a message,

And a lesson to teach.

Best is the chitter chatter,

Not as song or a speech,

But to speak with each other,

Everyone speaks I wonder why,

Let us find out let's just try.

Tarini Neeal

12.8.2016 (Age 9)

If there was any occasion to talk about my life, I would like people to think of me as in the following description. I strive to live up to these ideals, anyway I will strive to the end, for my life to match what I have said below.

…**Devendra,** born to **Vidya** and **Madan Mohan Jain** on September 13, 1941.

"He was judgemental, abrasive, impatient, not to mention inconsistent.

You know what his problem was? He took life so seriously. He was simply boring.

He knew what he wanted to say but that is not the same as how to say.

He ran a business and he made sure it was fair to all concerned.

He would do unto others what he would have liked others do unto him.

He had no regrets, that people did not understand him. But he knew that was their problem, not his.

He gave away money but more than that he gave away time and love that he knew money cannot buy.

He made a fool of himself many a times. He lived a life on his own terms.

Just to experience life. He went hiking/gliding/sky diving and para gliding.

He feared risk taking but risks he did take.

He would prepare well and then jump into the unknown.

After all, returns are directly proportional to the degree of risk taken."

And now as tears subside, I find it so amusing to
hear who this Devendra was, Wherever I am.

With thanks to **Frank Sinatra,** because it was
inspired by his song of similar narration and **Robin
Sharma,** whose book *"Who will cry when you are
gone"* gave me the idea to write my obituary and
then try and live to those ideals.

Biographical Note

Devendra Jain a chemist by training, not believing in Ph.D moved to England (1965) to work in advanced chemical labs. He worked for 5 years at **ICI Ltd.'s** corporate research centre and made his mark there. He worked for a further 12 years for **ICI** in India.

In 1982 he quit his job to start a small business. He is passionate for frugal innovation and an ardent supporter of use of Lateral Thinking skills.

After two successful businesses **Manas** and **Pluss,** he says *"Since mid-2022 I have embarked on starting a new business based on bamboos as raw materials. This enterprise promises to be a rerun of my first dream but in a much shorter time span"*. He is 82 now.

Apart from business he enjoys tending to his vast collection of Bonsais that is a hobby turning into professional skill, and teaching adults 3Rs. This book is his learnings of the past 50+ years, celebration of life with wife Tripti of 55 years. He is blessed with children Samit and Anu.

"I owe great debt to my parents - my mother Vidya and at a different level my father, Madan Mohan. Their unspoken but felt wisdom was the great advantage I had. The varied interests that my father had made a mark on my career as well. He acquired sketching skills at Triveni Kala Sangam. He was also a voracious reader. He played tennis and helped at Lajpat Bhawan with social service. His love for yoga touched me early in life."

Persons related to the author

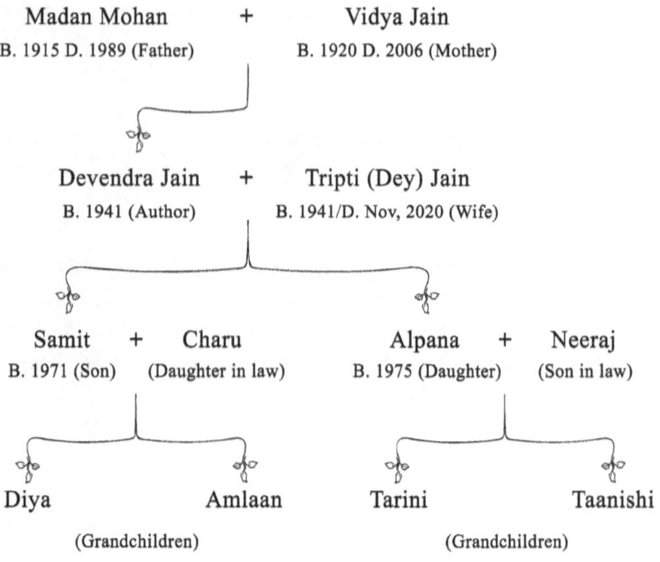

Friends and colleagues at work

Isaac Goodman - My Boss (and Guru) at ICI Ltd. 1966 - 1970.

Mannar Mannan - Colleague at Cosmo Films.

Atul Baijal - Colleague at Cosmo Films.

Anil Mehta - Colleague at Cosmo Films, and Co-founder of Pluss.

Sunil Ghanekar - Colleague at Cosmo Films.

Mausiji - Mother's sister.

Titiksha - Cousin.

Afterword

One liners in the book are like lamp posts in a dark night. I could be under any lamp post and the book will take me around the mini universe of ideas dispersed as if in a circle. Most difficult part was to decide which 40 odd ideas were too common and made less contribution to my life's learning. By removing those, I hope I was able to spare the reader what they may have come across elsewhere.

No life is so sacred that I would have had only unique experiences. But I do have here a unique set of ideas that I have followed again beginning in my 82nd year of life for starting a new business. It is unique and it challenged me to learn art and other soft skills. However, what I found was that this new start needed even more learning compared to the previous life covered in this book. I invite the reader to engage with me in a discussion on the subject via my email id **djain41@gmail.com**.